SEATTLE KRAKEN

BY ETHAN OLSON

Book design by Maggie Villaume
Cover design by Maggie Villaume

Photographs ©: Ted S. Warren/AP Images, cover, 4–5, 7, 8, 12, 15, 27; Elaine Thompson/AP Images, 10–11, 16–17; Nick Wass/AP Images, 19; Mark Humphrey/AP Images, 21; John Froschauer/AP Images, 23, 24–25; Lindsey Wasson/AP Images, 28

Press Box Books, an imprint of Press Room Editions.

ISBN
978-1-63494-681-0 (library bound)
978-1-63494-705-3 (paperback)
978-1-63494-751-0 (epub)
978-1-63494-729-9 (hosted ebook)

Library of Congress Control Number: 2022919587

Distributed by North Star Editions, Inc.
2297 Waters Drive
Mendota Heights, MN 55120
www.northstareditions.com

Printed in the United States of America
Mankato, MN
082023

ABOUT THE AUTHOR

Ethan Olson is a sportswriter and editor based in Minneapolis.

TABLE OF
CONTENTS

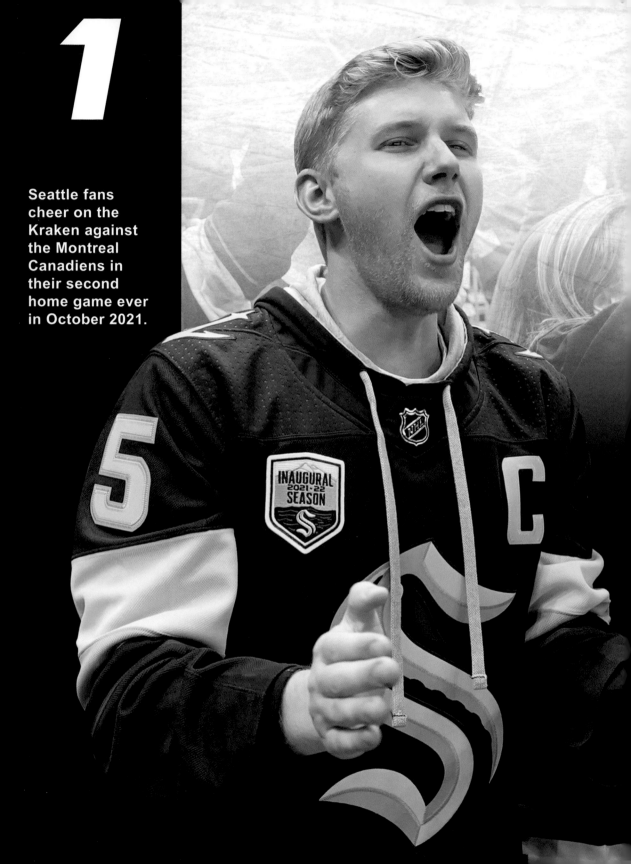

1

Seattle fans cheer on the Kraken against the Montreal Canadiens in their second home game ever in October 2021.

WELCOME TO *SEATTLE*

The sold-out Climate Pledge Arena was buzzing. It was only the second home game of the Seattle Kraken's first National Hockey League (NHL) season in 2021–22. The Kraken had lost five of their first six games. But the fans were still excited about their new team. The Montreal Canadiens were in town. And the Kraken wasted no time getting on the board. Seattle right winger

Jordan Eberle scored barely a minute into the game.

The teams started the second period with the Kraken leading 2–1. Seven minutes into the period, the Kraken struck again. The Canadiens were working to get into the Seattle zone. Kraken defenseman Jeremy Lauzon poked the puck past his team's blue line. His teammate Jaden Schwartz picked it up. Schwartz passed it ahead to Yanni Gourde. The center was zooming down the left wing. He skated toward the goal with the puck on his forehand. The Montreal goalie was fooled when Gourde switched to his backhand. That made it easy for Gourde to score his first goal with Seattle.

Jaden Schwartz brings the puck up the ice against the
Montreal Canadiens.

The Kraken were up the ice again
less than two minutes later. Seattle
defenseman Mark Giordano sent a long

A group of Kraken players salute the Seattle fans after their first home win.

pass to Gourde. The center got the puck on the left side of the ice again. Gourde passed it ahead to teammate

Brandon Tanev. The left winger got the puck in the middle of the ice. And he was ahead of the Montreal defense. Tanev fired a shot past the goalie for his second goal of the game. The Seattle fans erupted as their team went up 4–1.

Center Ryan Donato added another goal to put the Kraken up 5–1. The Seattle fans got to celebrate their team's first home win. And they hoped to see many more for years to come.

LOCAL SOUNDS

The Kraken's goal horn in the Climate Pledge Arena is inspired by Seattle. The team mounted a whistle from the *MV Hyak* inside the arena. The horn blasts after every Kraken goal. The *Hyak* was a local ferry that ran on the coastline of Washington from 1967 to 2019.

2

A Kraken flag flies atop the Space Needle in Seattle.

RELEASE THE
KRAKEN

The Kraken debuted in 2021–22. But Seattle already had a deep hockey history. The Seattle Metropolitans started playing in the Pacific Coast Hockey Association (PCHA) in 1915. The Metropolitans were a force. They won the PCHA's championship five times.

The Metropolitans even won the Stanley Cup in 1917. That made them the first American team to

Climate Pledge Arena is the renovated version of KeyArena, which was the longtime home of the National Basketball Association's Seattle SuperSonics.

win the famous trophy. But the PCHA shut down in 1924. Seattle would go almost 100 years without a professional hockey team. The city tried to bring an NHL team there for years. But the NHL wouldn't commit to Seattle. That changed in 2018. The city council approved $700 million to improve an arena already in Seattle. That was enough for the NHL to give Seattle its newest team.

In 2020, the team was officially named the Kraken. The name comes from a myth about a large sea creature. This creature looks similar to the giant Pacific octopus, which is found in the ocean waters near Seattle.

The Kraken's logo and colors fit with the water theme. Their jerseys are covered in different shades of blue. They also feature an *S* for the city of Seattle. That is also a call back to the Metropolitans. There was a red *S* in the middle of the Metropolitans' jerseys.

The hype around the Kraken rose quickly. When season tickets went on sale, fans were ready. The team received almost 33,000 requests for season tickets in the first few hours they were available. That was more than the team had available. Climate Pledge Arena held only 17,100 fans. Now it was time to build a team for the fans to support.

•CELEBRITY OWNERS

The Seattle Kraken are mostly owned by a group of businesspeople known as Seattle Hockey Partners. But a few other investors own small pieces of the team. Rapper Macklemore is one of them. Former Seattle Seahawks star running back Marshawn Lynch is another.

Former Seattle Seahawks star Marshawn Lynch is introduced at a Kraken game in April 2022.

3

Kraken coach
Dave Hakstol
waves to the
Seattle crowd
before their first
home game in
October 2021.

BUILDING A
TEAM

The Kraken needed players and coaches for their first season. Seattle hired Ron Francis to make those decisions. Francis had been the general manager of the Carolina Hurricanes. He also had a Hall of Fame career as a player. His experience helped him find talented players. Francis now had to build a team from scratch.

Francis hired Dave Hakstol to be the Kraken's first head coach.

That surprised the rest of the league. Hakstol had only 3.5 seasons of NHL head coaching experience. But during that time he had led the Philadelphia Flyers to the playoffs twice.

The NHL's expansion draft took place a month after Hakstol was hired. The Kraken were able to find a group of solid players for the 2021–22 season. Veteran defenseman Mark Giordano became the team's first captain. The Kraken also selected fellow defenseman Vince Dunn. He ended up leading the team in assists in 2021–22.

Centers Jared McCann and Yanni Gourde led the Seattle attack for its opening season. The two combined for

Mark Giordano's lone season in Seattle was his 17th in the NHL.

98 points. Veteran winger Jordan Eberle added 44 points.

The Kraken thrilled fans from their very first NHL game. They fell behind 3–0 early in the second period to the Vegas Golden Knights. Seattle then rallied to tie the game before losing 4–3.

Two nights later, Seattle went to Nashville to take on the Predators. Once again, the Kraken fell behind early. But goals from McCann and left winger Brandon Tanev put Seattle up 2–1 after

•EXPERIENCE NEEDED

Mark Giordano was one of Seattle's first players. The 38-year-old had been the Calgary Flames' captain for eight years. Giordano won the Mark Messier NHL Leadership Award in 2019–20 with the Flames. That award goes to a player who shows great leadership on and off the ice.

Brandon Tanev celebrates after scoring against the Nashville Predators in an October 2021 game.

the first period. Seattle held on this time and got its first win, 4–3. And 12 days after that, the Kraken earned their first home win by defeating the Montreal Canadiens.

VINCE DUNN

Vince Dunn started his NHL career with the St. Louis Blues. The defenseman showed promise there. And he helped St. Louis win the Stanley Cup in 2019. But the Blues were stacked with defensive talent. Minutes were hard to come by for Dunn.

Going to a new team solved that problem. The Kraken selected Dunn in the 2021 expansion draft. His role grew with Seattle. Dunn's strong play made him a key player in the Kraken's opening season. His 28 assists led the Kraken. Dunn only got better in his second year with the team. His 50 assists led the team once again. And his 64 points were the second-most for the Kraken. It was clear Seattle had a star defenseman to build around for years to come.

Vince Dunn's 14 goals in the 2022–23 season were twice as many as he'd scored in his first year with the Kraken.

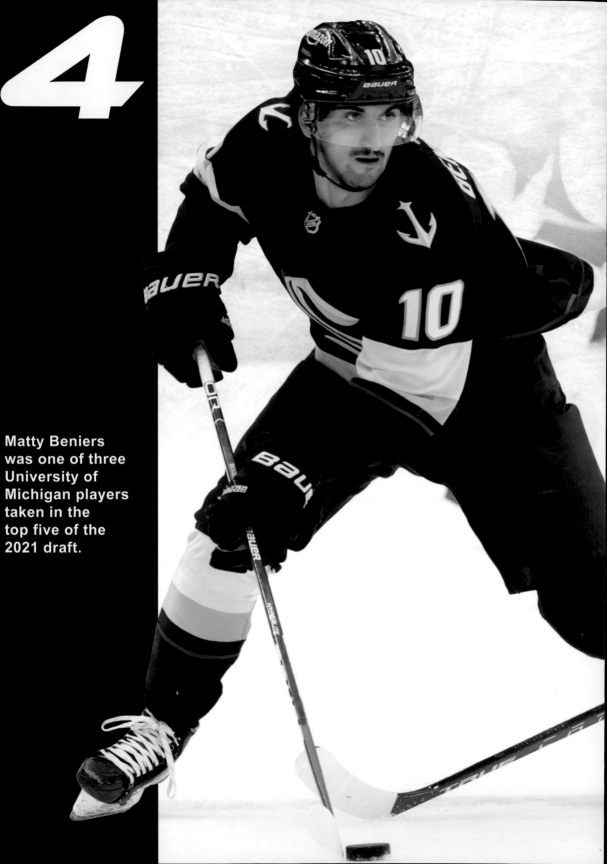

4

Matty Beniers was one of three University of Michigan players taken in the top five of the 2021 draft.

BRIGHT
FUTURE

The 2021–22 season was a building block for the Kraken. The young team did not have high expectations. The Kraken finished last in the Pacific Division. They ended up winning just 27 of their 82 games.

What made life harder for the Kraken was that one of their best players didn't debut until late in the season. The Kraken selected Matty Beniers with the second pick in the

2021 draft. Beniers decided to finish his sophomore season at the University of Michigan. Then he signed with the Kraken in April 2022. The 19-year-old center made an impact right away. He played the last 10 games of the season. Beniers tallied nine points in those games.

Despite Seattle not winning often, the fans stuck with their team. The Kraken sold out all their home games in 2021–22.

That fan base was treated to a much better season in 2022–23. The Kraken

•RISING STAR

Matty Beniers did more than make his NHL debut in 2022. Earlier that year he also played for Team USA at the Winter Olympics in Beijing, China. Beniers played in four games for the United States. He tallied a goal and an assist. The Americans finished fifth in the tournament.

Kraken players celebrate with Jared McCann (far left) after he scored against the San Jose Sharks in an April 2022 game.

surpassed their 2021–22 win total in their 47th game. By April 6, 2023, the Kraken had a chance to clinch their first playoff berth in front of their home crowd.

The Kraken salute their home fans after clinching a spot in the playoffs for the first time.

The Kraken faced the Arizona Coyotes. Jared McCann scored in the first period to give Seattle the lead. Vince Dunn and Jordan Eberle added goals in the second period. With the Kraken ahead 4–1 in the third, fans rose to their feet. They roared as the clock ticked down to zero. Seattle was heading to the playoffs!

In the first round, the Kraken took on the Colorado Avalanche. The Avalanche were the defending champions. If the Kraken were intimidated, they didn't show it. The series went to Game 7. Seattle right winger Oliver Bjorkstrand scored twice to lead his team to victory. Kraken fans couldn't wait to see what the future held.

SEATTLE KRAKEN
QUICK STATS

FOUNDED: 2021

STANLEY CUP CHAMPIONSHIPS: 0*

KEY COACH:

Dave Hakstol (2021–): 73 wins, 77 losses, 14 overtime losses

HOME ARENA: Climate Pledge Arena (Seattle, WA)

MOST CAREER POINTS: Jared McCann (120)

MOST CAREER GOALS: Jared McCann (67)

MOST CAREER ASSISTS: Vince Dunn (78)

MOST CAREER SHUTOUTS: Martin Jones (3)

Stats are accurate through the 2022–23 season.

GLOSSARY

ASSIST

A pass, rebound, or deflection that results in a goal.

CAPTAIN

A player who serves as the leader of a team.

DEBUT

To make a first appearance.

DRAFT

An event that allows teams to choose new players coming into a league.

EXPANSION DRAFT

A draft that allows a new team to fill their roster with players already in the league.

INVESTORS

People or organizations that put money into financial plans.

VETERAN

A player who has spent several years in a league.

TO LEARN MORE

BOOKS

Davidson, B. Keith. *NHL*. New York: Crabtree Publishing, 2022.

Doeden, Matt. *G.O.A.T. Hockey Teams*. Minneapolis: Lerner Publications, 2021.

Duling, Kaitlyn. *Women in Hockey*. Lake Elmo, MN: Focus Readers, 2020.

MORE INFORMATION

To learn more about the Seattle Kraken, go to **pressboxbooks.com/AllAccess**.

These links are routinely monitored and updated to provide the most current information available.

INDEX